M000168996

SHOULD THIS OCTOPUS HAVE FEWER LEGS?

And 25 Other Funny Signs for People to Ponder, Post, and Rip Away

PJ McQuade

adamsmedia
Avon, Massachusetts

Copyright © 2013 by F+W Media, Inc.
All rights reserved.
This book, or parts thereof, may not be reproduced in any
form without permission from the publisher; exceptions are
made for brief excerpts used in published reviews.

Published by
Adams Media, a division of F+W Media, Inc.
57 Littlefield Street, Avon, MA 02322. U.S.A.
www.adamsmedia.com

ISBN 10: 1-4405-5757-8
ISBN 13: 978-1-4405-5757-6

Printed in China.

10 9 8 7 6 5 4 3 2 1

Some of the illustrations in this book employ drawings of easily recognized
celebrities, culturally iconic fictional characters, or other images that
may be legally claimed by third parties. This book was not authorized,
approved, licensed, or endorsed by any such third party. All rights to the
materials that served as resources for these illustrations are fully reserved
by the various entities who own these rights.

Many of the designations used by manufacturers and sellers to distinguish
their product are claimed as trademarks. Where those designations
appear in this book and F+W Media was aware of a trademark claim, the
designations have been printed with initial capital letters.

Illustrated by PJ McQuade.

*This book is available at quantity discounts for bulk purchases.
For information, please call 1-800-289-0963.*

Dedicated to Daria

FOREWORD

During my travels across this great land, I have encountered many a funny thing. Balloon animals. Cat videos. Lemurs. Donald Trump.

But nothing compares to the moment I encountered a rather strange telephone pole–flyer in Tuscaloosa. On it was a picture of Lionel Richie. "Hello?" it read, "Is it me you're looking for?" A bubbly sense of euphoria overtook my body and split my sides with laughter.

I have spent my days since then desperately scouring the globe for more of these hanging treasures but, alas, have only come upon them in the wild once in a very blue moon.

And so I have taken it upon myself to create this book, *Should This Octopus Have Fewer Legs?*, the most motley collection of funny signs ever assembled, all for your viewing pleasure. In this collection you'll find new takes on old classics, homages to your favorite movies, and straight-up hilarious notices that'll keep you in stitches.

I mean, where else are you going to find a Wanted poster for Santa Claus? Or a guide to making The World's Smallest Paper Airplane?

But listen up—because here's where it really gets good. This is not a pick-up and put-down book. Oh no. You have a responsibility to spread the word. You are hereby charged with ripping these posters out and posting them wherever you see fit.

You know you want to. Maybe you're tired of walking past that same old LOST CAT sign that's been posted at your bus stop for the last five years. And those NEED A TUTOR? signs all over college campuses are so played out.

It's time to make a change; time to spice things up. Pick a poster and grab a pair of scissors. Cut along the dotted lines to remove the poster from the book, then cut along each tab. And BAM! You're ready to work some magic. Grab some tape, a stapler, even a tube of Super Glue if you're fearless. What needs a douse of the funny? Your wall? A telephone pole? Your best friend's back?

And what if all these amusing signs get you inspired? Turn to the back of *Should This Octopus Have Fewer Legs?* for some blank templates. You can take pen to paper and make your own hilarious posters.

Later, when you stroll by and see your handy work, or hear someone at the bus stop chuckling as they rip off an octopus leg, you'll know that you made the world more interesting, and hopefully a little more euphoric.

ENJOY and go forth!

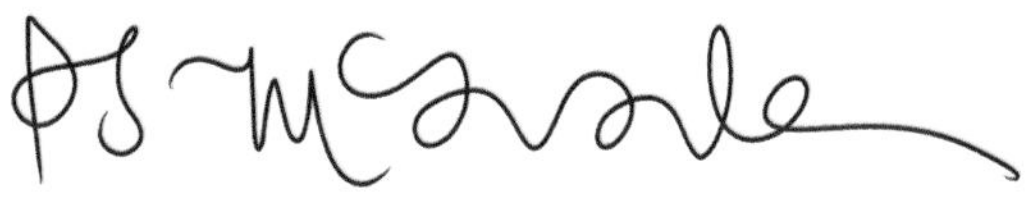

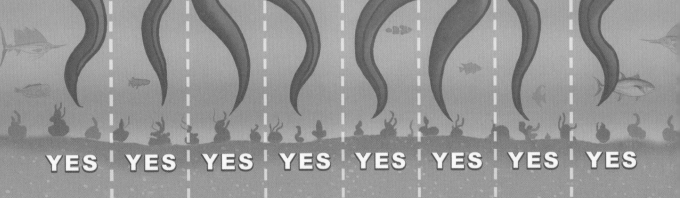

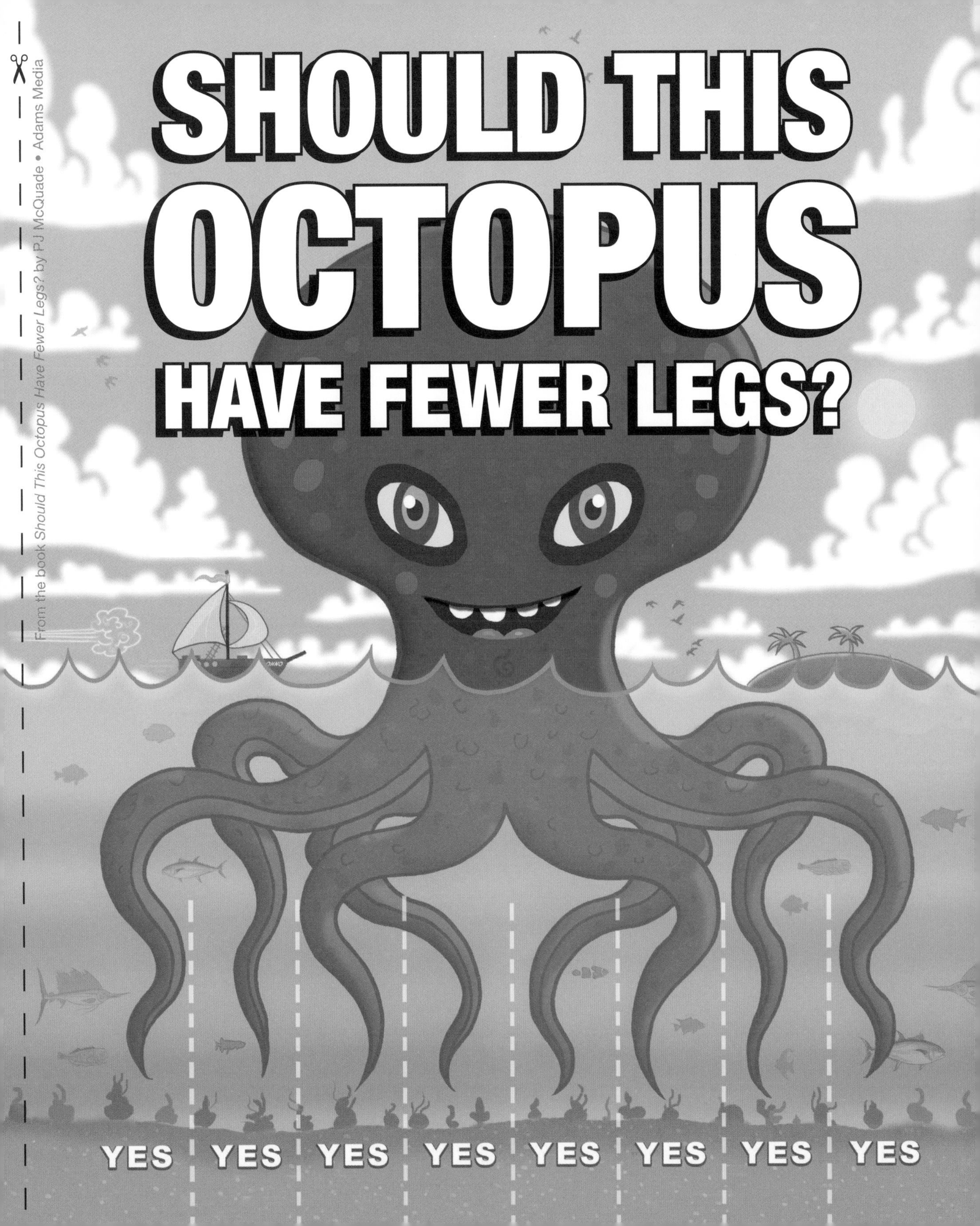

From the book *Should This Octopus Have Fewer Legs?* by PJ McQuade • Adams Media

MAKE THE WORLD'S SMALLEST
PAPER AIRPLANE

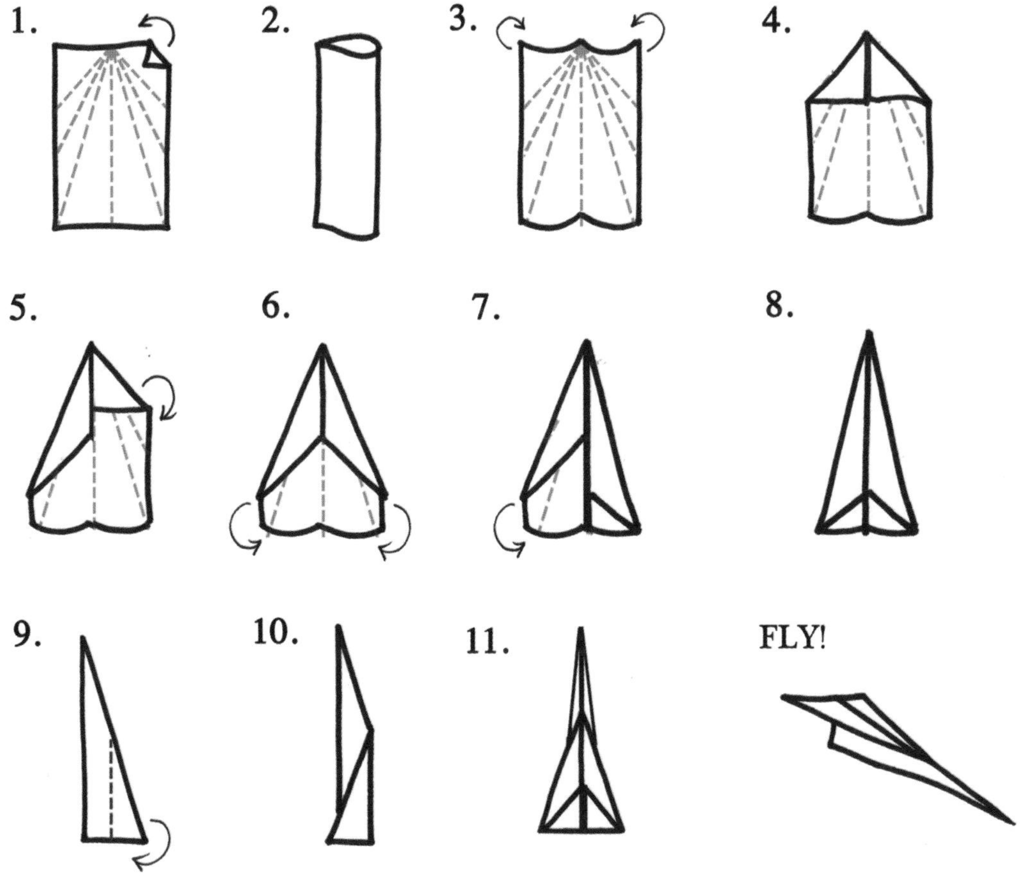
1.
2.
3.
4.
5.
6.
7.
8.
9.
10.
11.
FLY!

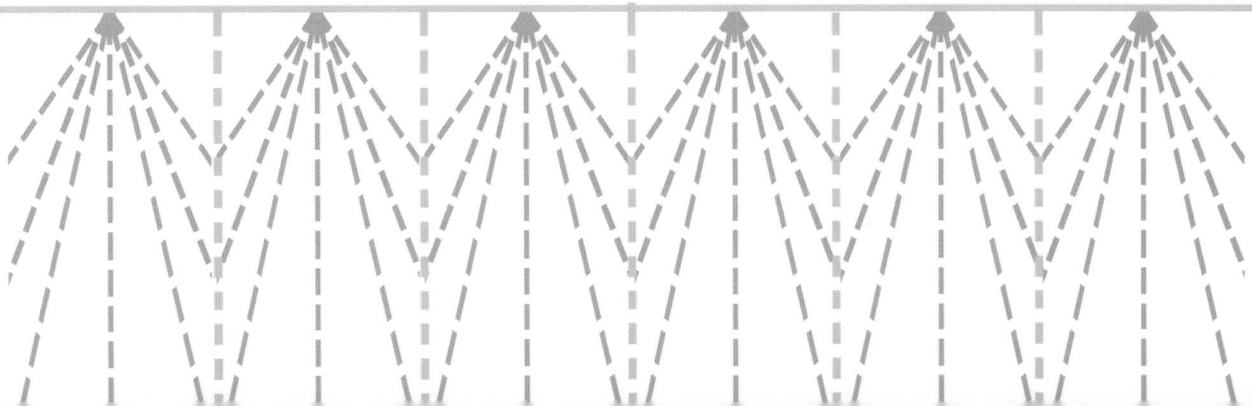

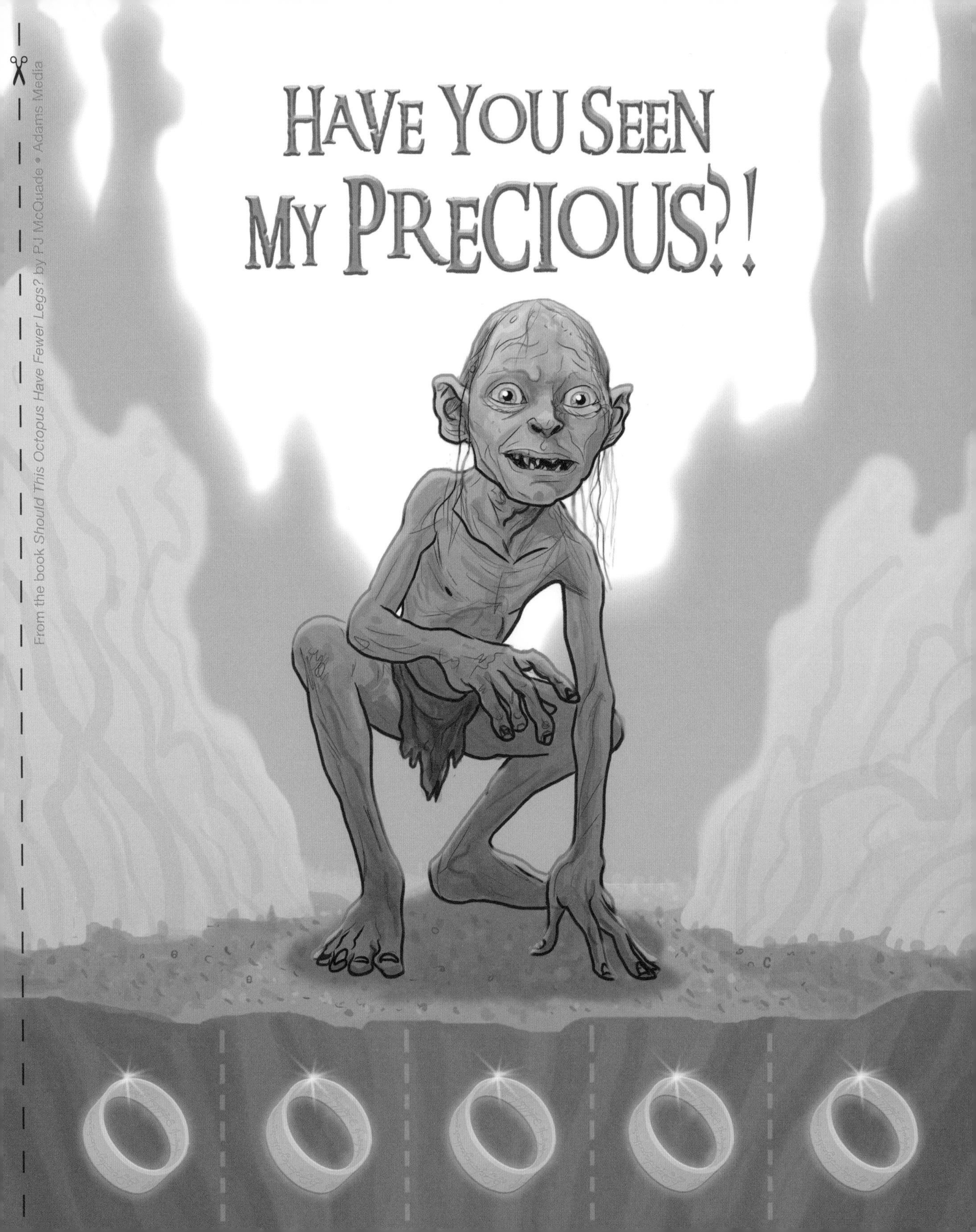
HAVE YOU SEEN
MY PRECIOUS?!

From the book *Should This Octopus Have Fewer Legs?* by PJ McQuade • Adams Media

WANTED

BREAKING & ENTERING

DO NOT
BE FOOLED
- BY THIS -
CHARLATAN
HE IS UP TO
NO GOOD!

$$ REWARD $$
SEVEN SCHILLINGS
—— and a ——
C H R I S T M A S
G O O S E
for any information
L E A D I N G   T O
HIS CAPTURE!

BEWARE
HE HAS BEEN
SEEN
ON FIRE ESCAPES
& ROOFTOPS
LATE AT NIGHT
- IN YOUR -
NEIGHBORHOOD
ENTERS THROUGH
YOUR CHIMNEY
and WINDOWS.
HE WILL STEAL
your VALUABLES
& EAT ALL of
YOUR COOKIES!

THE RED-SUITED THIEF!

E. SCROOGE 555-1843
E. SCROOGE 555-1843
E. SCROOGE 555-1843
E. SCROOGE 555-1843
E. SCROOGE 555-1843
E. SCROOGE 555-1843
E. SCROOGE 555-1843
E. SCROOGE 555-1843

Pin the Tail on the Donkey

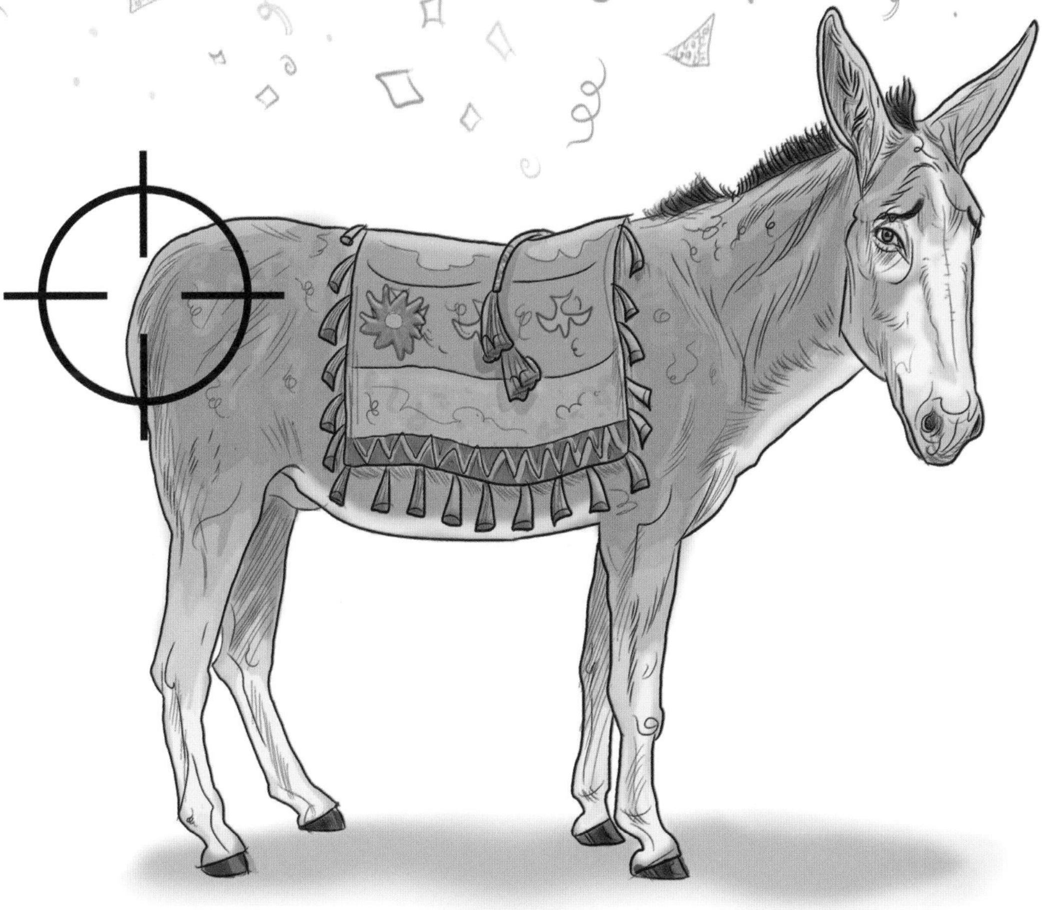

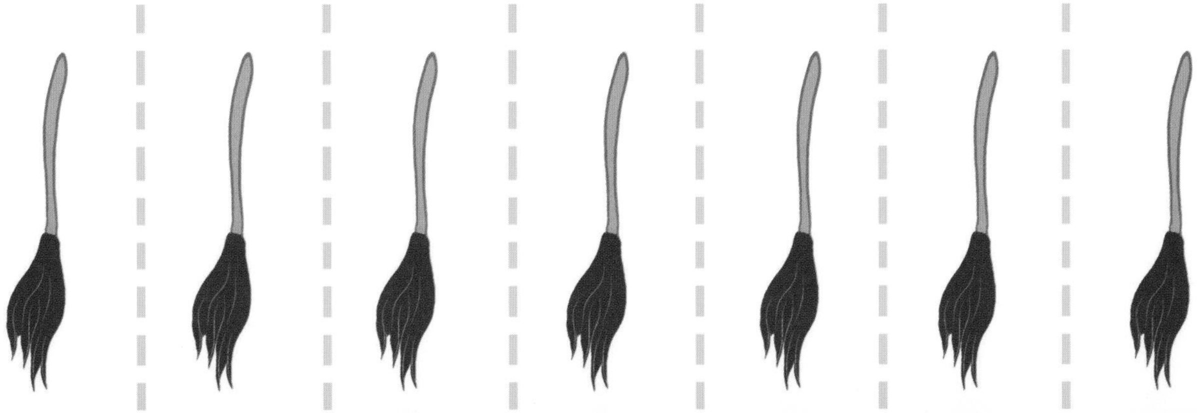

From the book *Should This Octopus Have Fewer Legs?* by PJ McQuade • Adams Media

From the book *Should This Octopus Have Fewer Legs?* by PJ McQuade • Adams Media

SEEKING NEW ROOMMATE

SYM, quiet, easily frustrated, world weary, book lover seeks roommate for basement apt. on Sesame Street. I enjoy paperclip and bottle-cap collecting and cooking oatmeal. Looking for a quiet, non-intrusive, rational-minded person or muppet who keeps to themselves.

$800/month plus utilities & half of the cable bill. Background check & income verification required.

ABSOLUTELY
NO SAXOPHONES
NO RUBBER DUCKIES
PIGEON FRIENDLY

BERT 555-1234   BERT 555-1234   BERT 555-1234   BERT 555-1234   BERT 555-1234   BERT 555-1234   BERT 555-1234

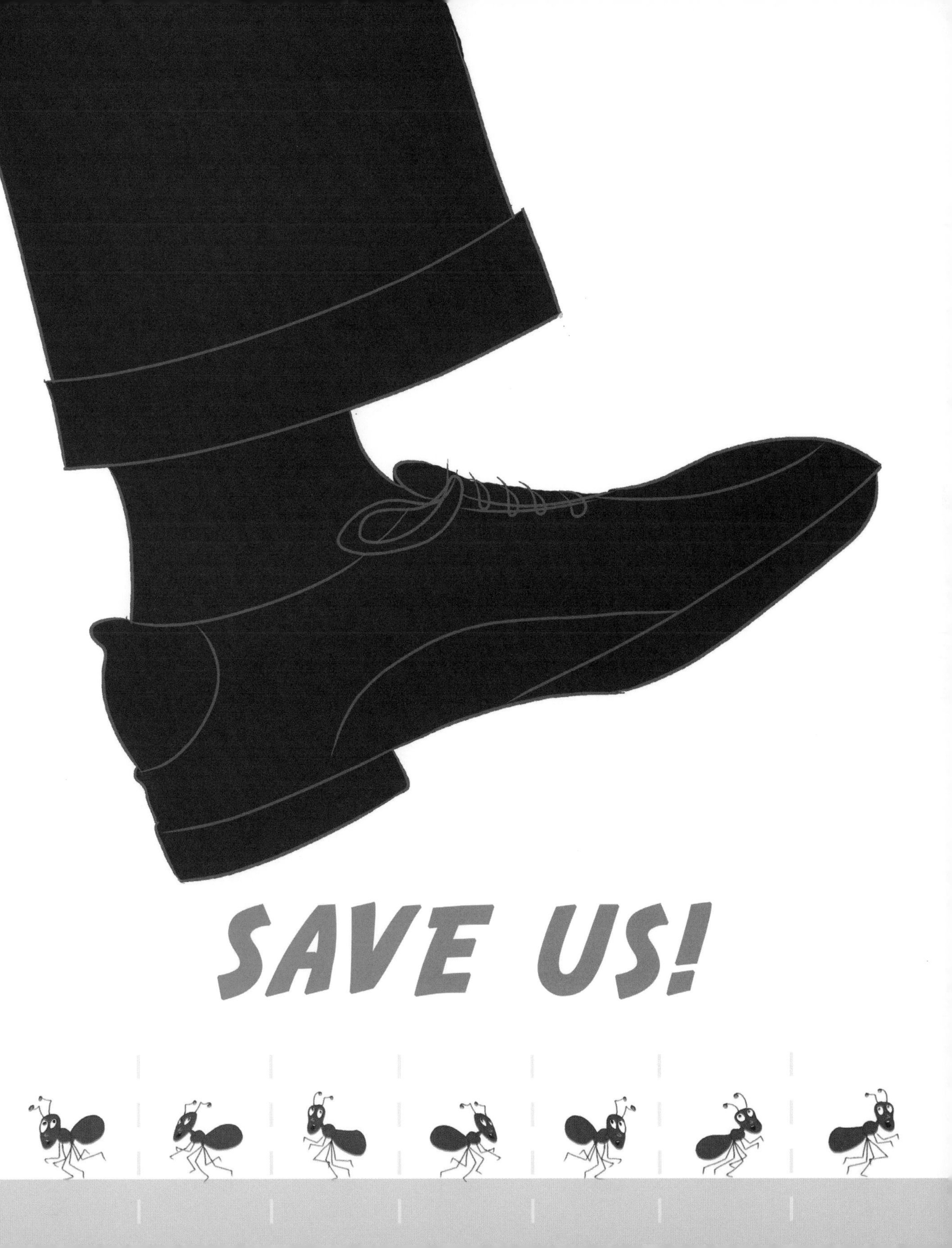
SAVE US!

From the book *Should This Octopus Have Fewer Legs?* by PJ McQuade • Adams Media

DAGOBAH INC. PRESENTS
YODA'S LANGUAGE LESSONS
TODAY SIGN UP YOU WILL!

LEARN YOU CAN
TUSKEN, HUTTESE, WOOKIEE-SPEAK, THE TRIBAL TONGUE OF EWOKS, JAWANESE, MANDALORIAN, DROID, & MANY, MANY MORE!

OFFICES LOCATED IN THE DAGOBAH SYSTEM. OUTER RIM TERRITORIES, SULIUS SECTOR, IN A HUT NEAR THE SWAMP.

GUARANTEED, YOUR SATISFACTION IS!

TODAY SIGN UP YOU WILL
YODA-1-800

TODAY SIGN UP YOU WILL
YODA-1-800

TODAY SIGN UP YOU WILL
YODA-1-800

TODAY SIGN UP YOU WILL
YODA-1-800

TODAY SIGN UP YOU WILL
YODA-1-800

TODAY SIGN UP YOU WILL
YODA-1-800

TODAY SIGN UP YOU WILL
YODA-1-800

TODAY SIGN UP YOU WILL
YODA-1-800

From the book *Should This Octopus Have Fewer Legs?* by PJ McQuade • Adams Media

LOST SLIPPER

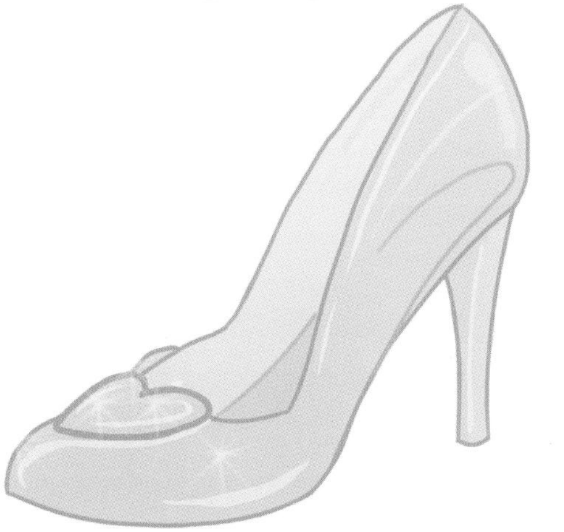

FOUND JUST AFTER THE STROKE OF MIDNIGHT ON THE STEPS OF ROYAL BALL. DESPERATELY SEEKING THE OWNER. MUST FIT PERFECTLY.

P. CHARMING 555-3457

P. CHARMING 555-3457

P. CHARMING 555-3457

P. CHARMING 555-3457

P. CHARMING 555-3457

P. CHARMING 555-3457

P. CHARMING 555-3457

P. CHARMING 555-3457

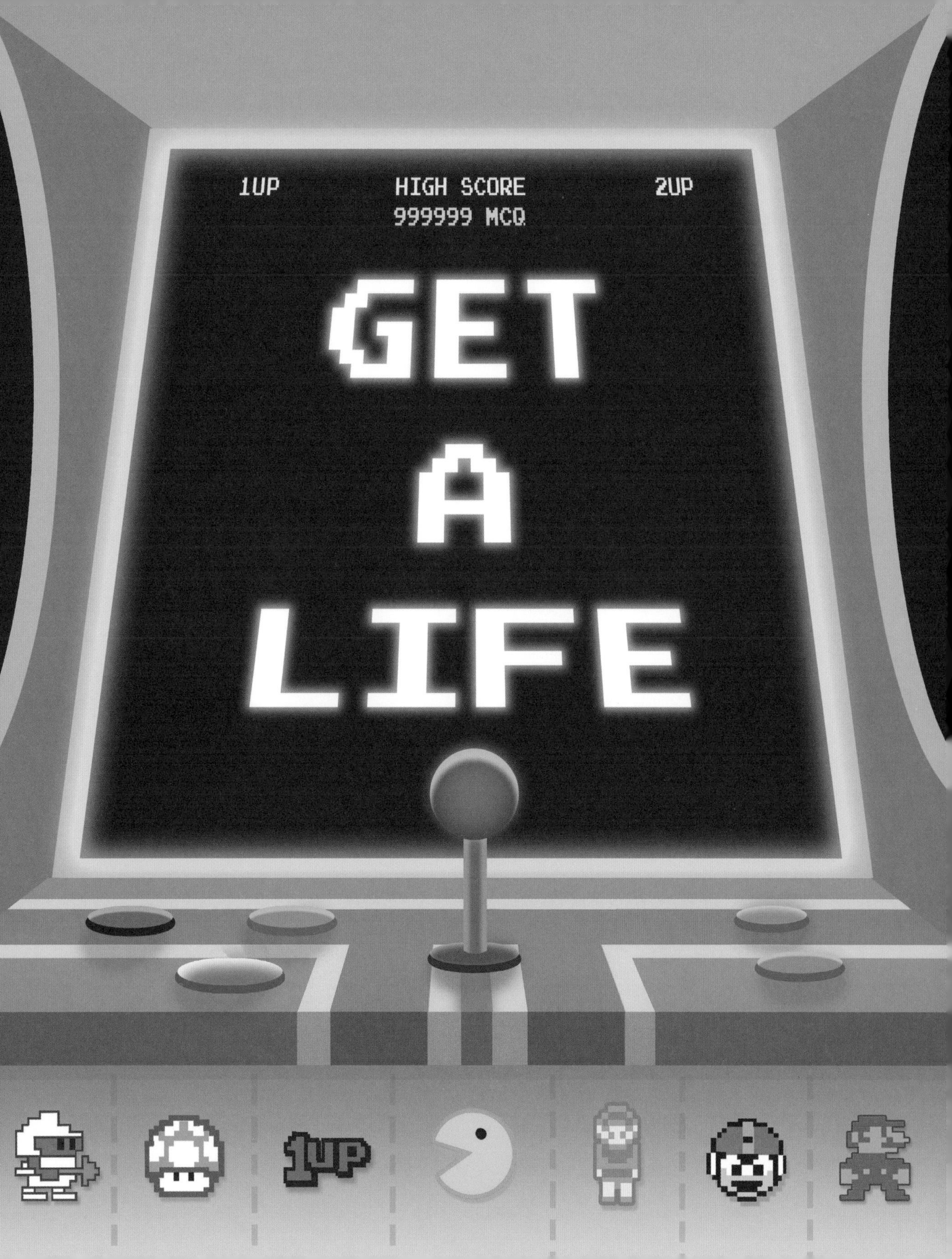
1UP
HIGH SCORE
999999 MCQ
2UP
GET
A
LIFE
1UP

HAVE A HEART

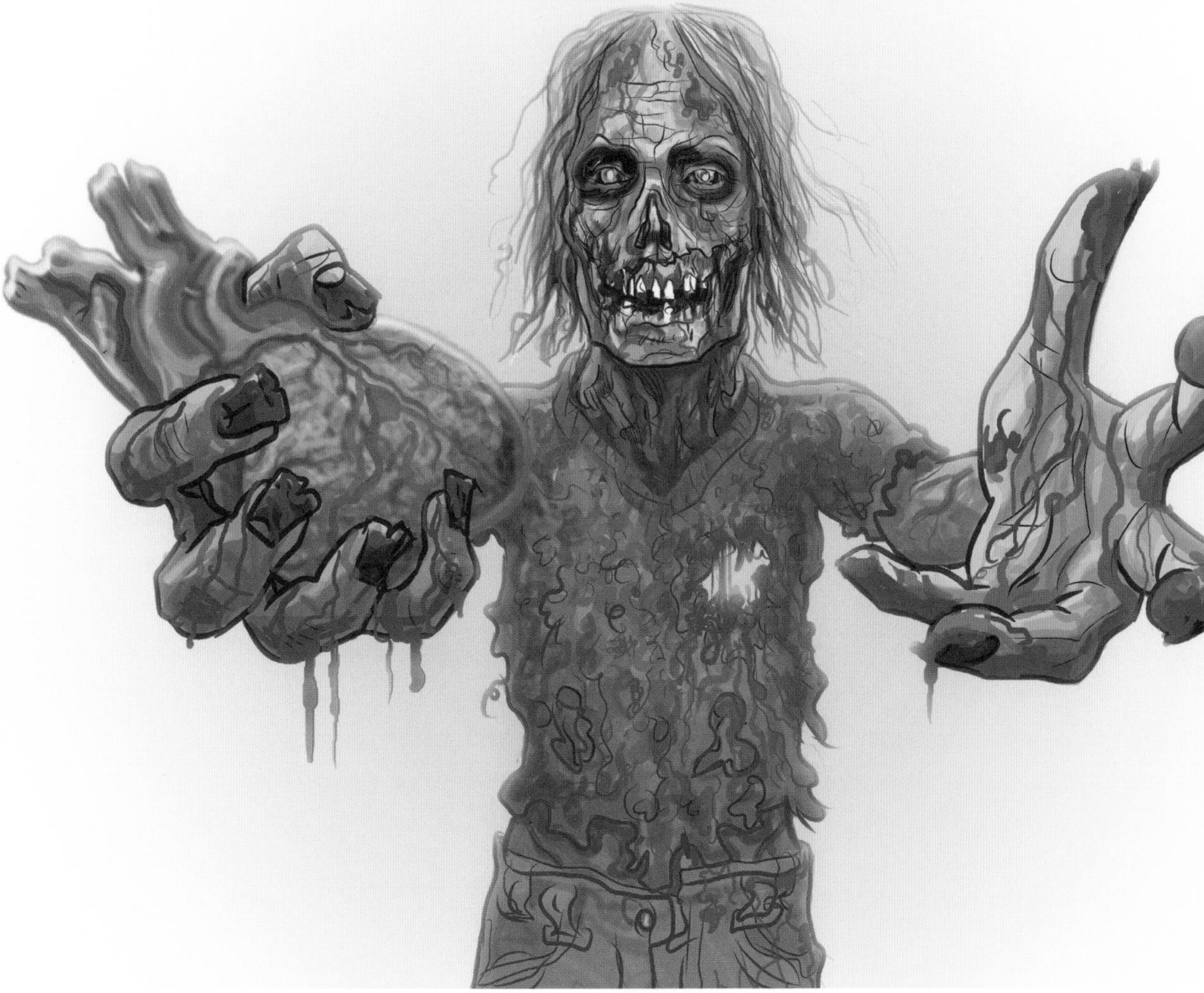

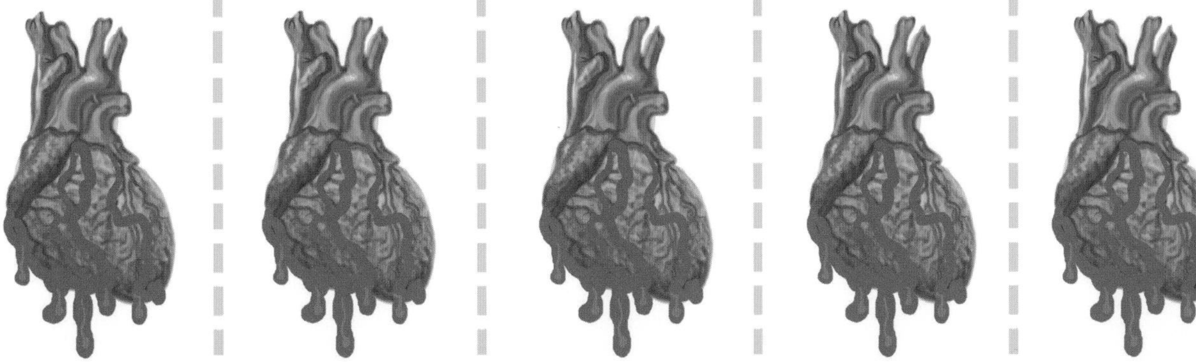

From the book *Should This Octopus Have Fewer Legs?* by PJ McQuade • Adams Media

✂

From the book *Should This Octopus Have Fewer Legs?* by PJ McQuade • Adams Media

FREE
BACON
STRIPS

From the book *Should This Octopus Have Fewer Legs?* by PJ McQuade • Adams Media

Need A Hand?

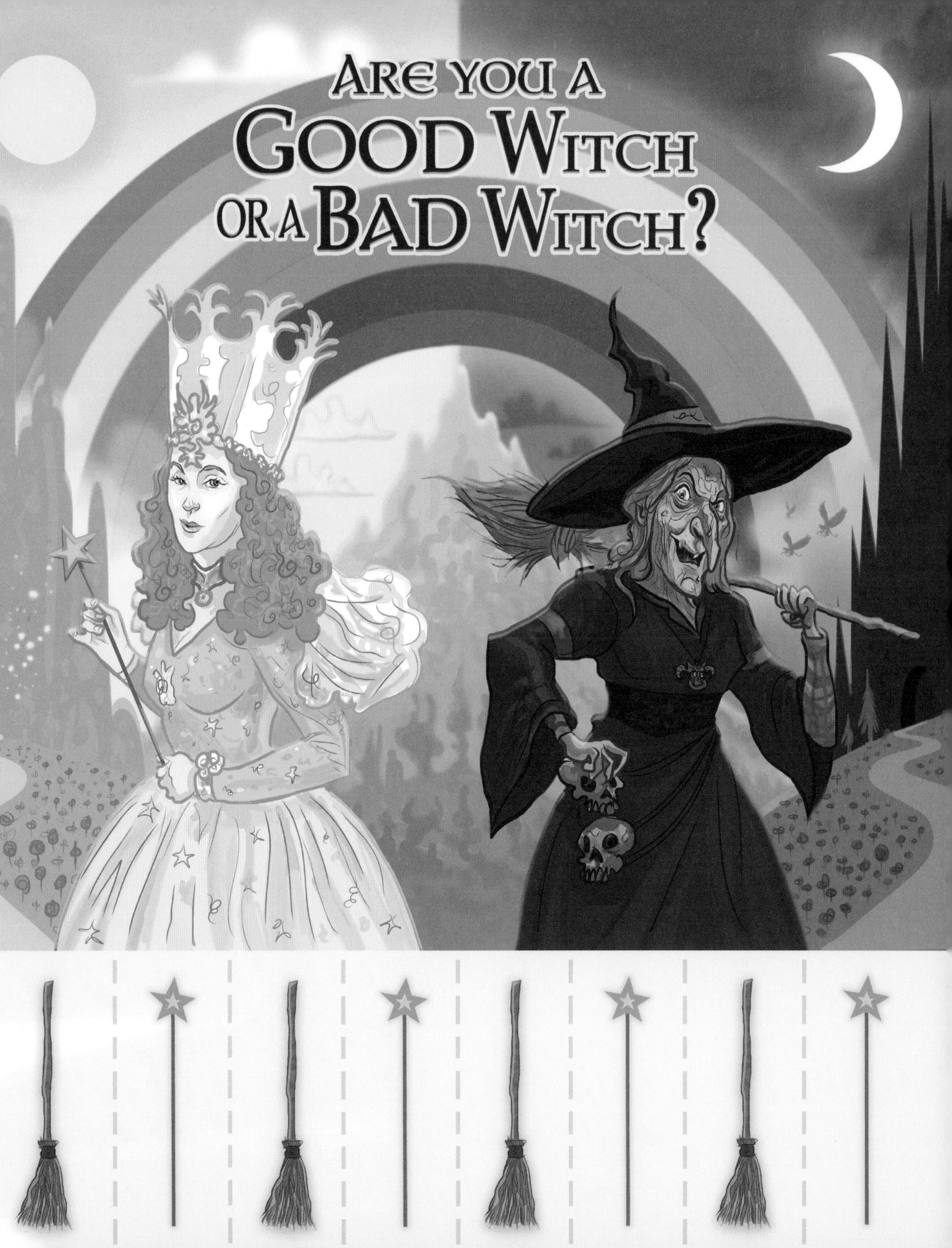
ARE YOU A
GOOD WITCH
OR A BAD WITCH?

WHO DOESN'T LIKE A FREEBEE?

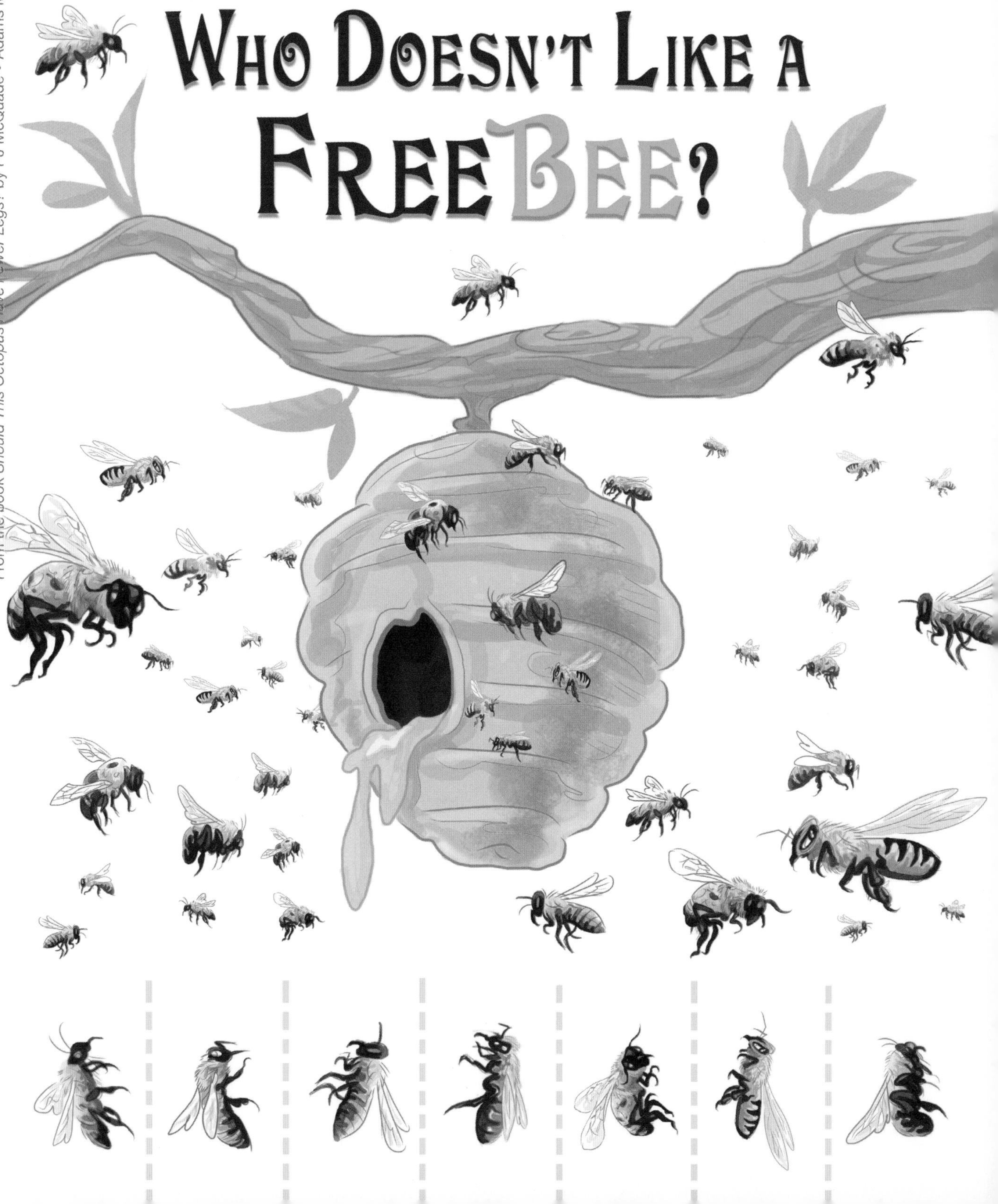

From the book *Should This Octopus Have Fewer Legs?* by PJ McQuade • Adams Media

From the book *Should This Octopus Have Fewer Legs?* by PJ McQuade • Adams Media

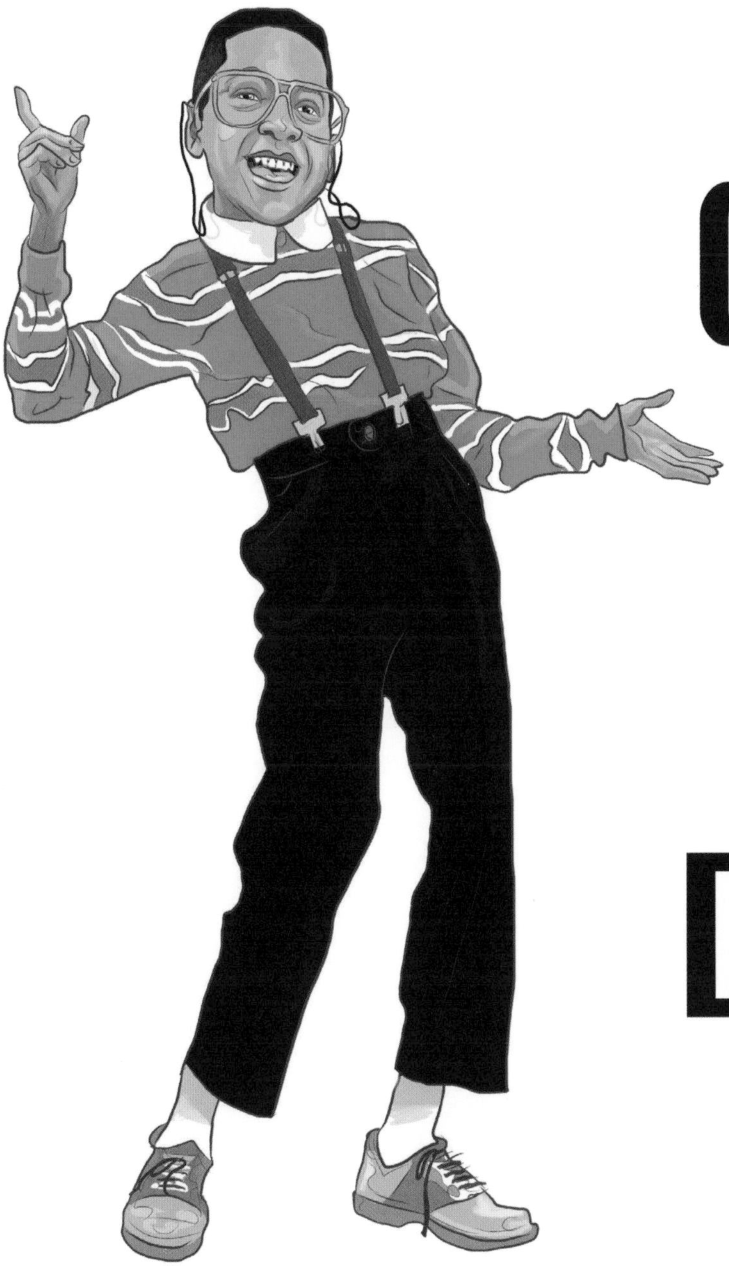

CAN'T GET A DATE?

FEB 1ØTH

OCT 3RD

JUNE 19TH

MAY 30TH

FEB 13TH

APRIL 26TH

DEC 5TH

MAY 8TH

From the book *Should This Octopus Have Fewer Legs?* by PJ McQuade • Adams Media

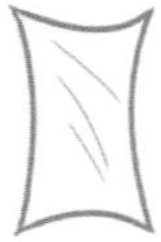 WIN

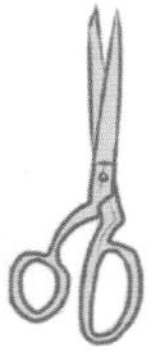 LOSE

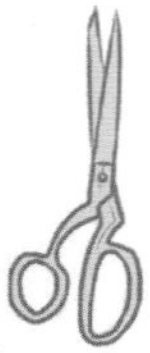 WIN

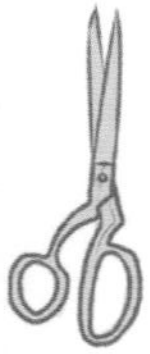 DRAW

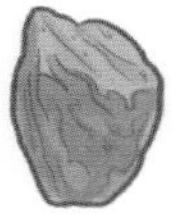 WIN

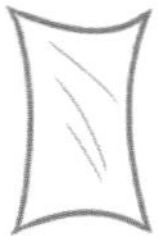 LOSE

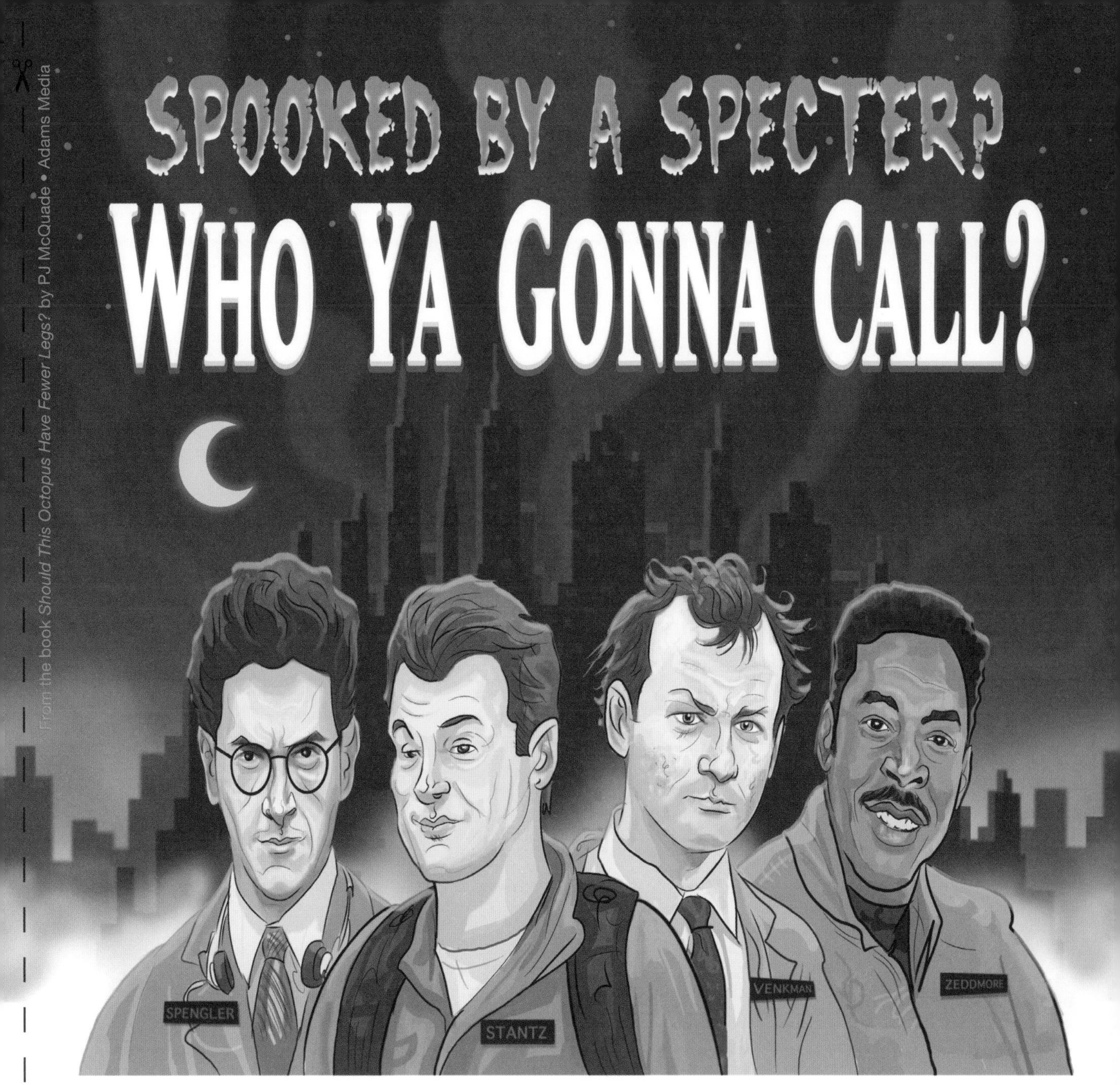

SPOOKED BY A SPECTER?
WHO YA GONNA CALL?
SPENGLER
STANTZ
VENKMAN
ZEDDMORE

GHOSTBUSTERS (212)555-2368 WE'RE READY TO BELIEVE YOU

GHOSTBUSTERS (212)555-2368 WE'RE READY TO BELIEVE YOU

GHOSTBUSTERS (212)555-2368 WE'RE READY TO BELIEVE YOU

GHOSTBUSTERS (212)555-2368 WE'RE READY TO BELIEVE YOU

GHOSTBUSTERS (212)555-2368 WE'RE READY TO BELIEVE YOU

GHOSTBUSTERS (212)555-2368 WE'RE READY TO BELIEVE YOU

GHOSTBUSTERS (212)555-2368 WE'RE READY TO BELIEVE YOU

From the book *Should This Octopus Have Fewer Legs?* by PJ McQuade • Adams Media

From the book *Should This Octopus Have Fewer Legs?* by PJ McQuade • Adams Media

WHO SAYS YOU CAN'T TAKE A JOKE?

TAKE ONE!

WHAT'S A FROG'S
FAVORITE DRINK?
CROAK-A-COLA

WHAT'S FORREST GUMP'S
E-MAIL PASSWORD?
1FORREST1

WHAT DO FLIES WEAR
ON THEIR FEET?
SHOOS

WHAT'S LARGE, GRAY,
AND DOESN'T MATTER?
AN IRRELEPHANT

WHAT DOES A WICKED
CHICKEN LAY?
DEVILED EGGS

WHAT DO YOU CALL
SOMEONE ELSE'S CHEESE?
NACHO CHEESE

WHERE DO
POLAR BEARS VOTE?
THE NORTH POLL

WHAT'S BROWN
AND STICKY?
A STICK

FREE DENTAL WORK!

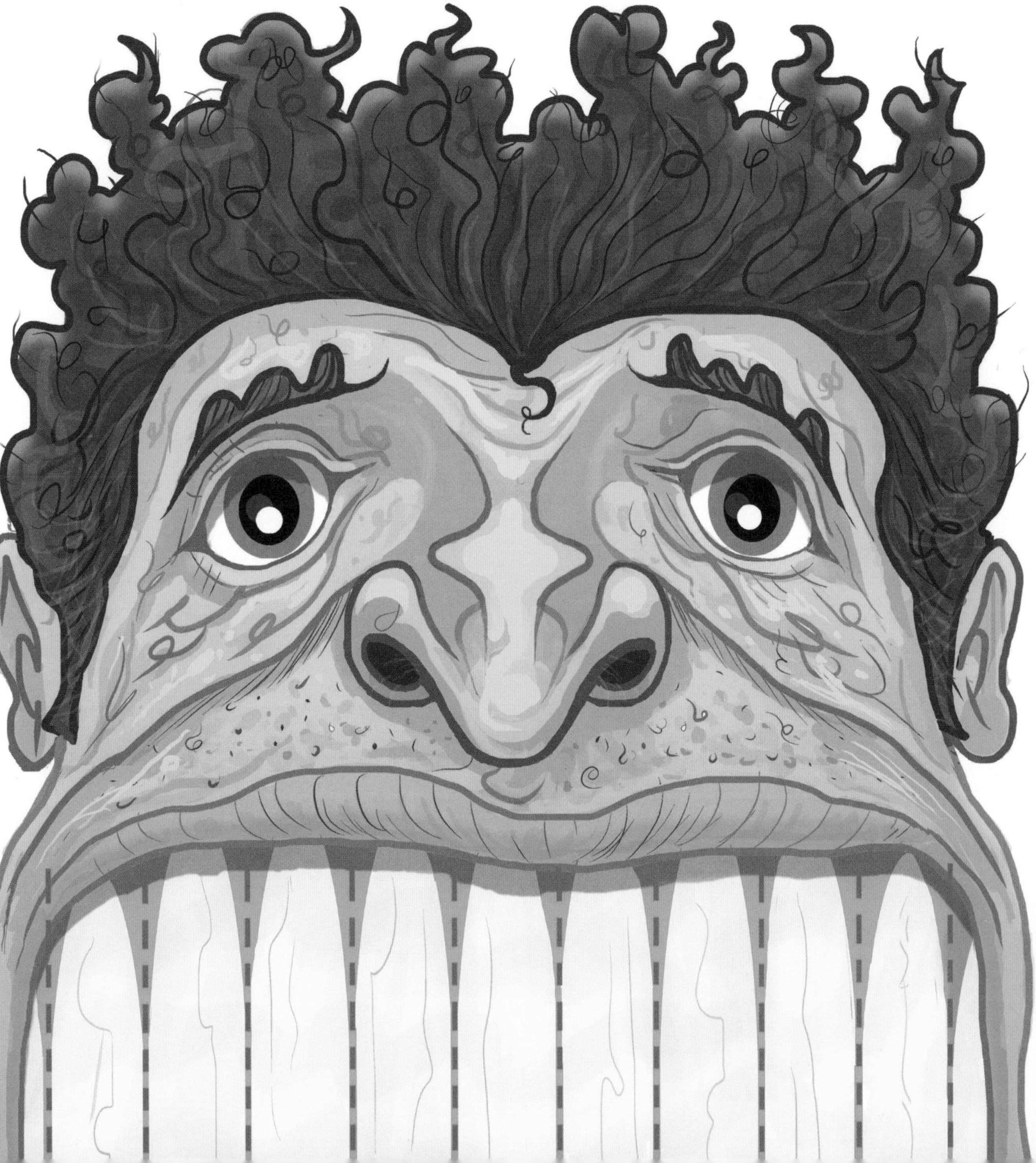

TAKE MY *Breath* AWAY

From the book *Should This Octopus Have Fewer Legs?* by PJ McQuade • Adams Media

Breath

Breath

Breath

Breath

Breath

Breath

Breath

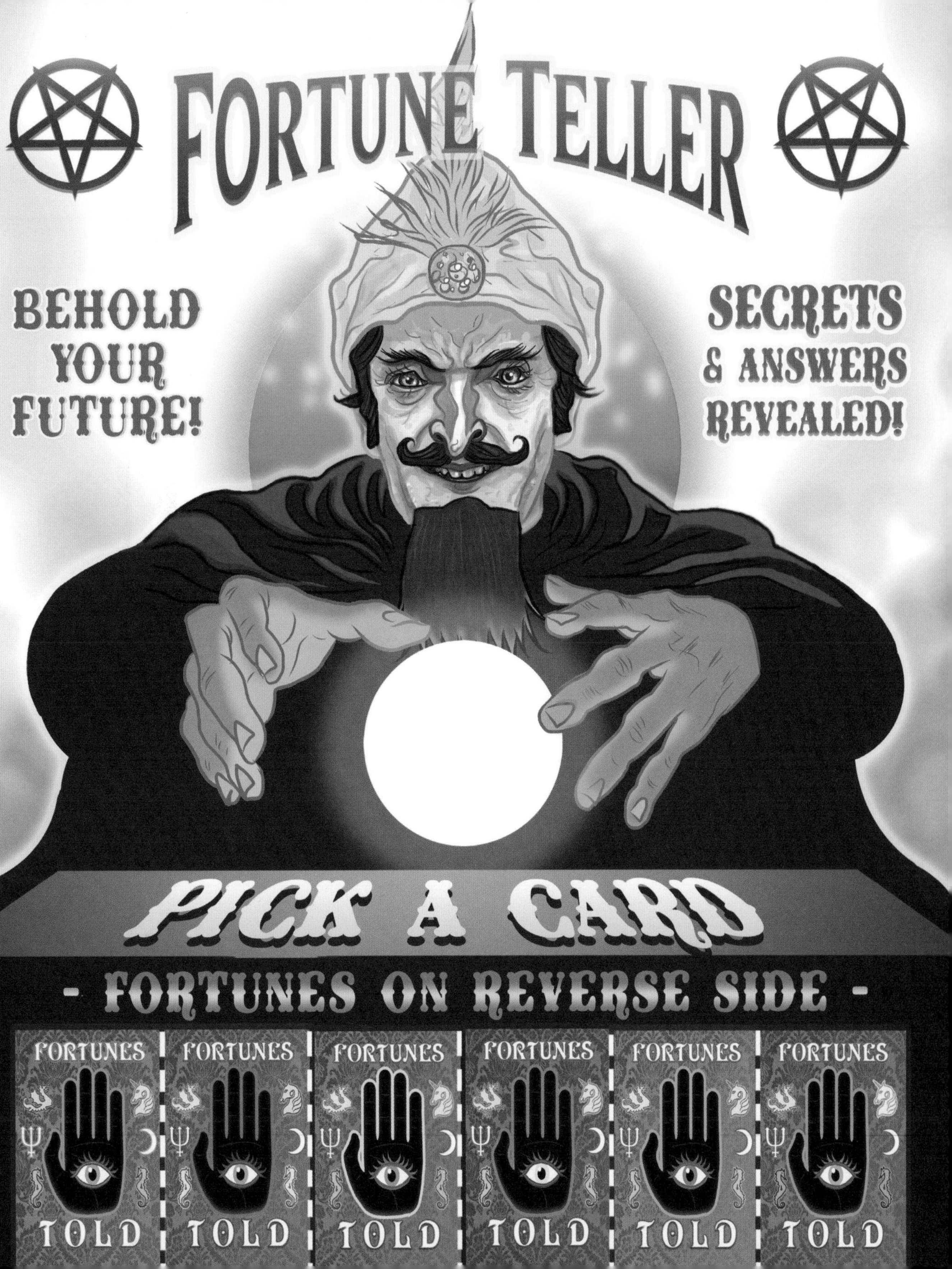
FORTUNE TELLER
BEHOLD YOUR FUTURE!
SECRETS & ANSWERS REVEALED!
PICK A CARD
- FORTUNES ON REVERSE SIDE -
FORTUNES TOLD
FORTUNES TOLD
FORTUNES TOLD
FORTUNES TOLD
FORTUNES TOLD
FORTUNES TOLD

| YOU ARE HAVING A GOOD HAIR DAY | HAPPINESS IS THE PERSON WITH A TINY PIECE OF PAPER IN POCKET | YOU HAVE A KNACK FOR FINDING GREAT FLIERS | TODAY IS THE 8TH DAY OF THE REST OF YOUR LIFE | THE SECRET TO LIFE LIES IN THE AVOIDANCE OF DEATH | YOU WILL MEET A VERY IMPORTANT STREET FLIER TODAY |

Hello?

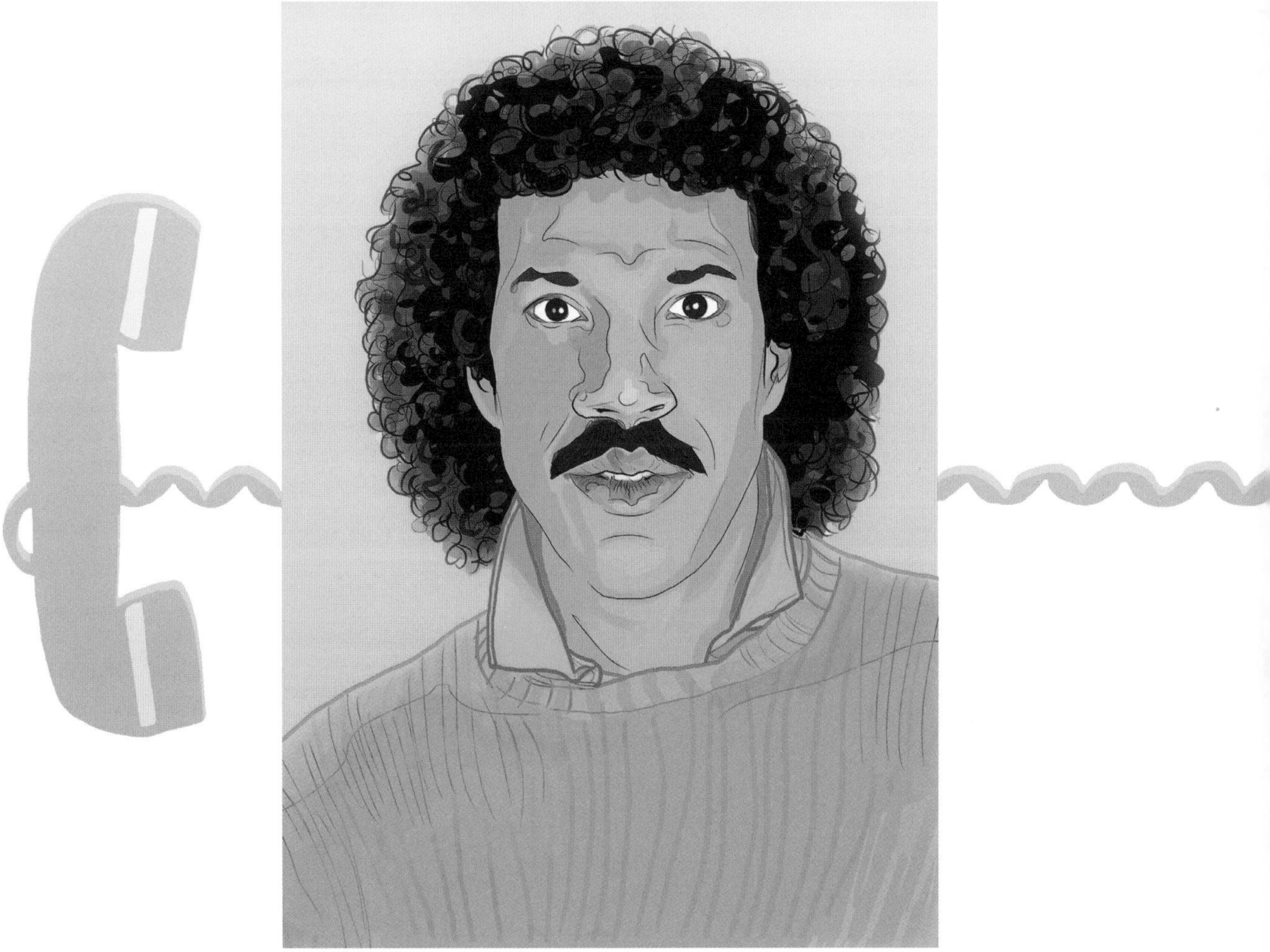

Is it me you're looking for?

I can see it in your eyes

I can see it in your smile

I want to tell you so much

I love you

I can see it in your eyes

I can see it in your smile

I want to tell you so much

I love you

From the book *Should This Octopus Have Fewer Legs?* by PJ McQuade • Adams Media

What's your SIGN?

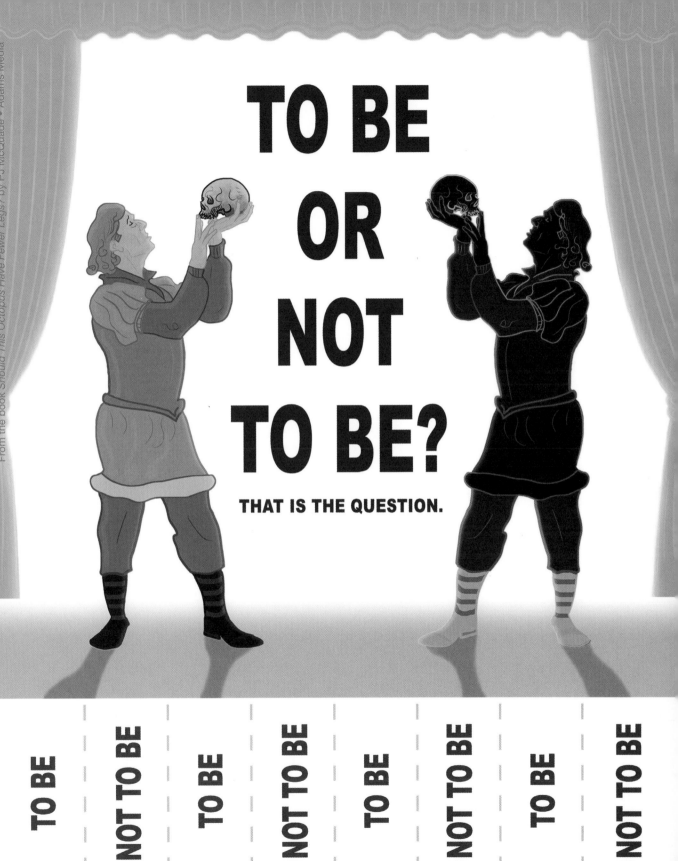

From the book Should This Octopus Have Fewer Legs? by PJ McQuade • Adams Media

BRIDGE FOR SALE

QUAINT SUSPENSION BRIDGE, LOCATED ON THE EAST RIVER OF NYC. WONDERFUL TRUSSES & STONEWORK. PRICE NEGOTIABLE. CALL FOR DETAILS.

BRING OWN TRUCK FOR PICKUP

1-800-BUY-BRIDGE
1-800-BUY-BRIDGE
1-800-BUY-BRIDGE
1-800-BUY-BRIDGE
1-800-BUY-BRIDGE
1-800-BUY-BRIDGE
1-800-BUY-BRIDGE
1-800-BUY-BRIDGE

From the book *Should This Octopus Have Fewer Legs?* by PJ McQuade • Adams Media

Which came first?

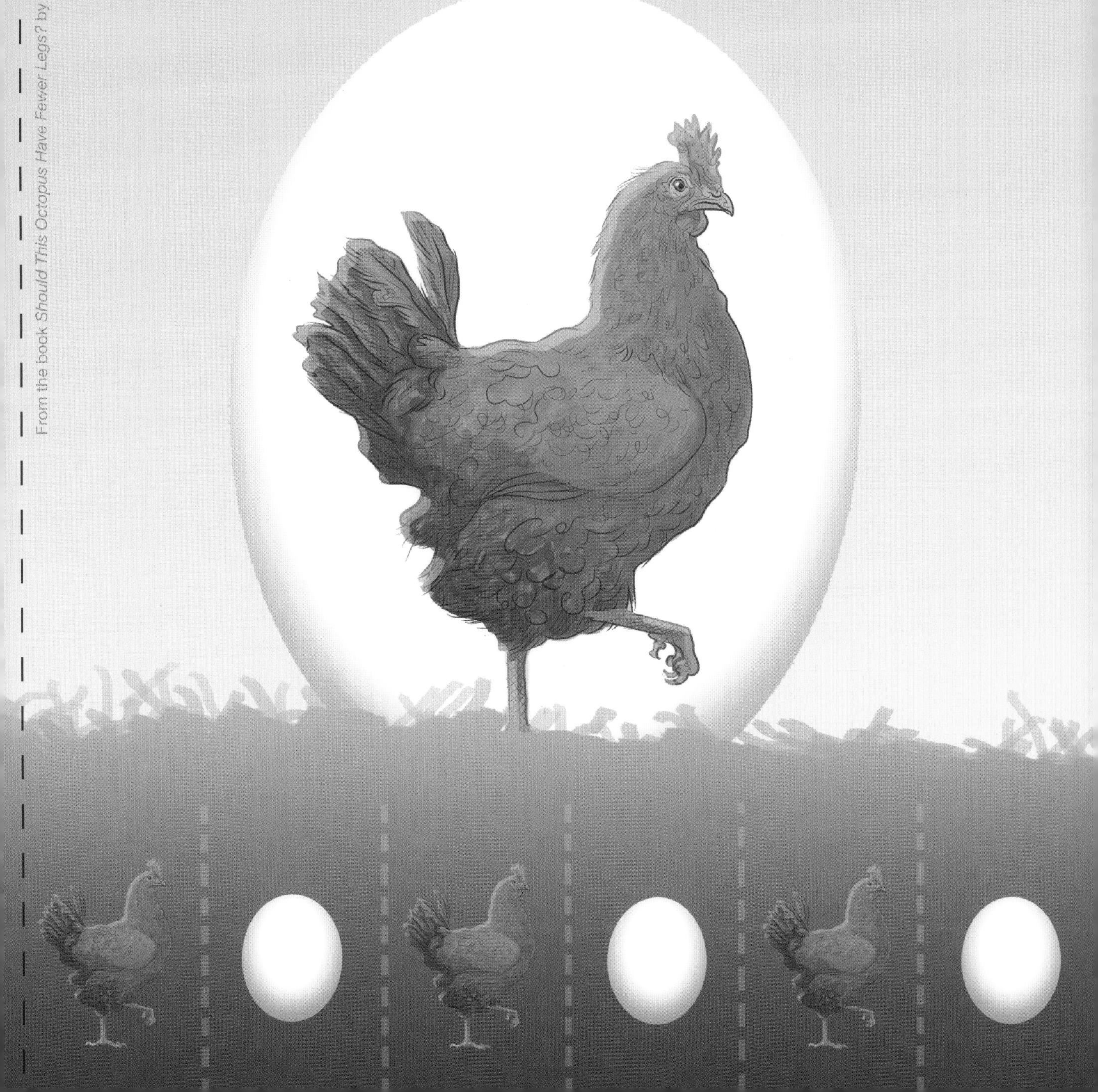

From the book *Should This Octopus Have Fewer Legs?* by PJ McQuade • Adams Media

From the book *Should This Octopus Have Fewer Legs?* by PJ McQuade • Adams Media

CAN'T GROW A

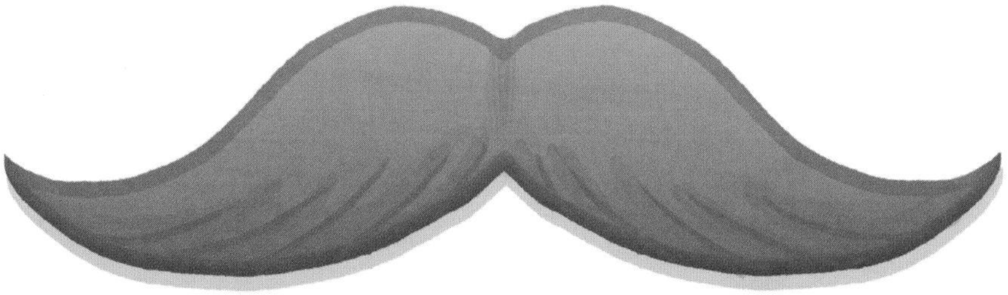

GO ON, TAKE A FREE MUSTACHE!

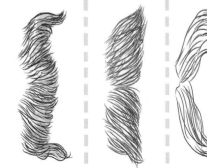

From the book *Should This Octopus Have Fewer Legs?* by PJ McQuade • Adams Media

Spice Up Your Life

OREGANO

MUSTARD
SEED

PAPRIKA

CINNAMON

BASIL

CURRY

From the book *Should This Octopus Have Fewer Legs?* by PJ McQuade • Adams Media

HELP!

I've Lost My Sheep!

I don't know where to find them!
PLEASE CALL

Miss Peep
406-555-7337

Miss Peep
406-555-7337

Miss Peep
406-555-7337

Miss Peep
406-555-7337

Miss Peep
406-555-7337

Miss Peep
406-555-7337

Miss Peep
406-555-7337

Miss Peep
406-555-7337

From the book *Should This Octopus Have Fewer Legs?* by PJ McQuade • Adams Media

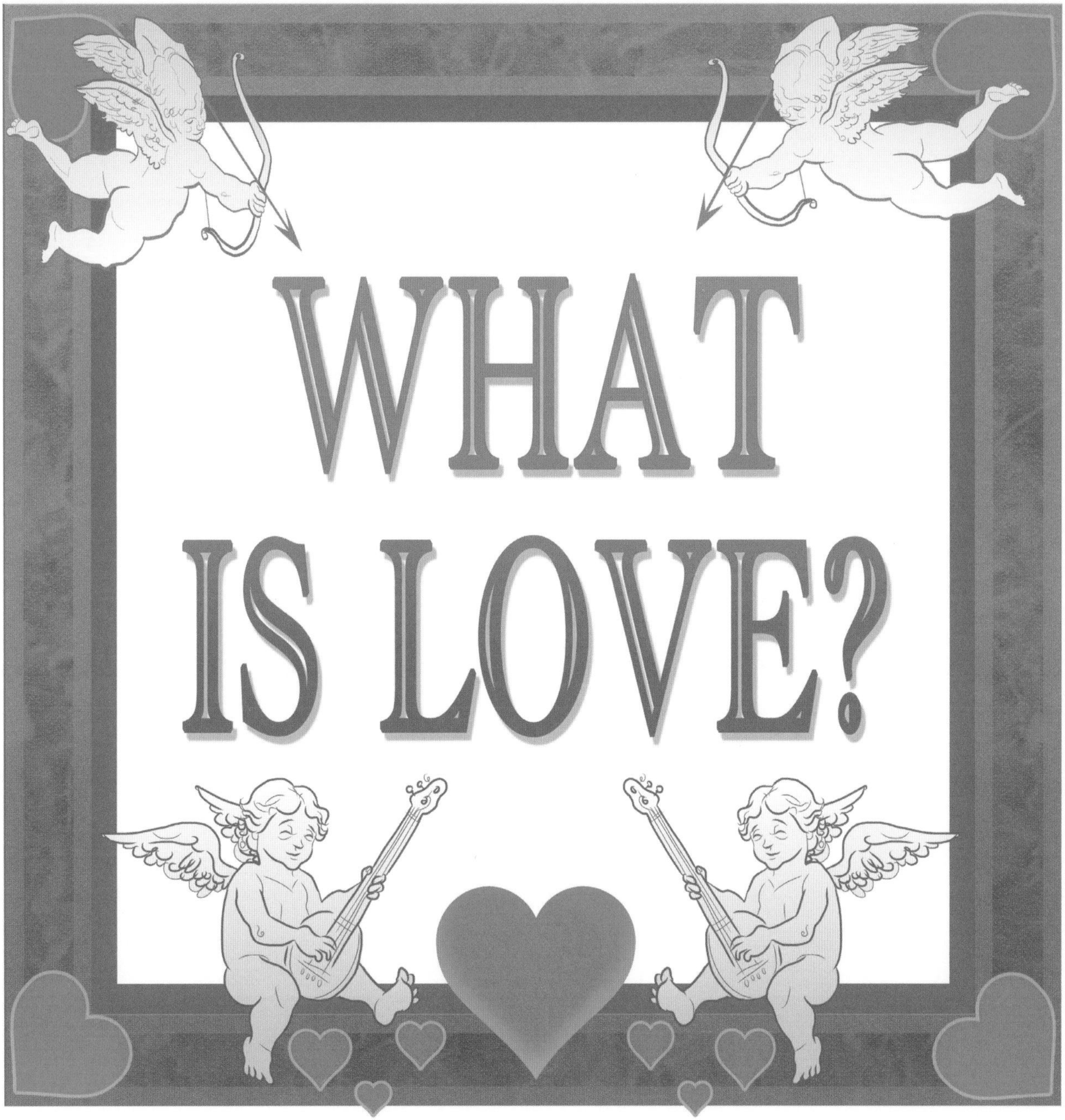
WHAT
IS LOVE?

Baby Don't Hurt Me, Don't Hurt Me, No More

Patient

Kind

A Battlefield

A Warm Puppy

A Four-Letter Word

I Want You to Show Me

From the book *Should This Octopus Have Fewer Legs?* by PJ McQuade • Adams Media

HANNIBAL LECTER'S
GUT-WRENCHING NEW COOKBOOK
Dying for Dinner

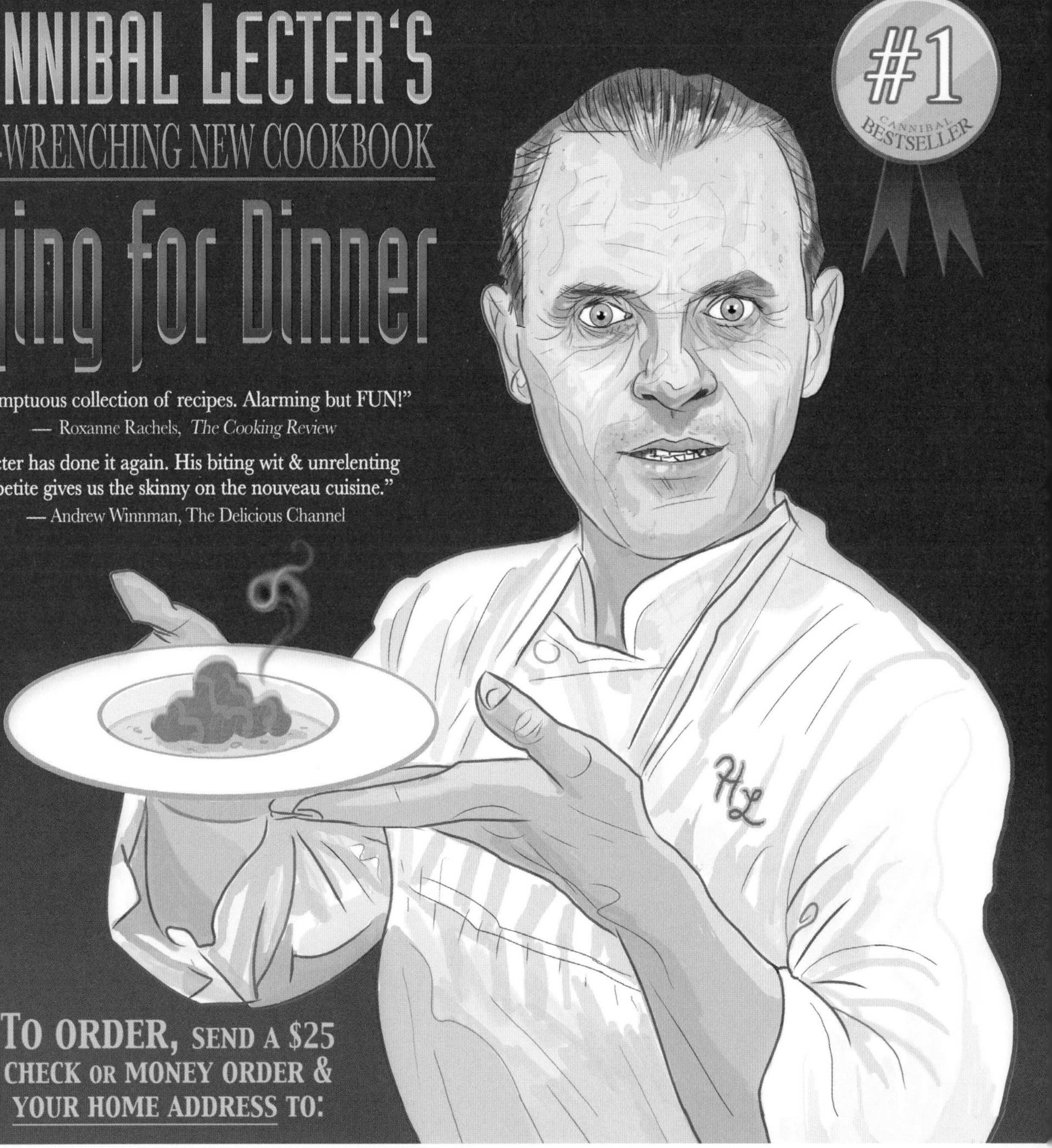
#1
CANNIBAL
BESTSELLER
HL

"A sumptuous collection of recipes. Alarming but FUN!"
— Roxanne Rachels, *The Cooking Review*

"Lecter has done it again. His biting wit & unrelenting appetite gives us the skinny on the nouveau cuisine."
— Andrew Winnman, The Delicious Channel

TO ORDER, SEND A $25 CHECK OR MONEY ORDER & YOUR HOME ADDRESS TO:

HANNIBAL LECTER'S
DYING FOR DINNER
The Baltimore State Hospital
for the Criminally Insane,
1989 Miss Mofet Lane,
Baltimore, MD 21201

HANNIBAL LECTER'S
DYING FOR DINNER
The Baltimore State Hospital
for the Criminally Insane,
1989 Miss Mofet Lane,
Baltimore, MD 21201

HANNIBAL LECTER'S
DYING FOR DINNER
The Baltimore State Hospital
for the Criminally Insane
1989 Miss Mofet Lane,
Baltimore, MD 21201

HANNIBAL LECTER'S
DYING FOR DINNER
The Baltimore State Hospital
for the Criminally Insane,
1989 Miss Mofet Lane,
Baltimore, MD 21201

HANNIBAL LECTER'S
DYING FOR DINNER
The Baltimore State Hospital
for the Criminally Insane,
1989 Miss Mofet Lane,
Baltimore, MD 21201

HANNIBAL LECTER'S
DYING FOR DINNER
The Baltimore State Hospital
for the Criminally Insane
1989 Miss Mofet Lane,
Baltimore, MD 21201

From the book *Should This Octopus Have Fewer Legs?* by PJ McQuade • Adams Media

Get a Clue

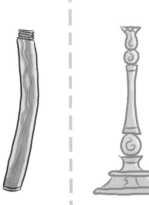
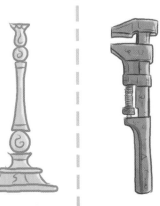

NICE ASS!

From the book *Should This Octopus Have Fewer Legs?* by PJ McQuade • Adams Media

I've never seen a cubicle as well organized as yours.

Your clothing choices always match your eyes & complement your body type.

I really appreciate your witty repartee.

You have an excellent ear for classical music.

Your recipe for bouillabaisse rivals those in the finest French restaurants.

Your Facebook updates are always informative and interesting.

From the book *Should This Octopus Have Fewer Legs?* by PJ McQuade • Adams Media

Who Can I Turn To?

867-5309 867-5309 867-5309 867-5309 867-5309 867-5309 867-5309 867-5309

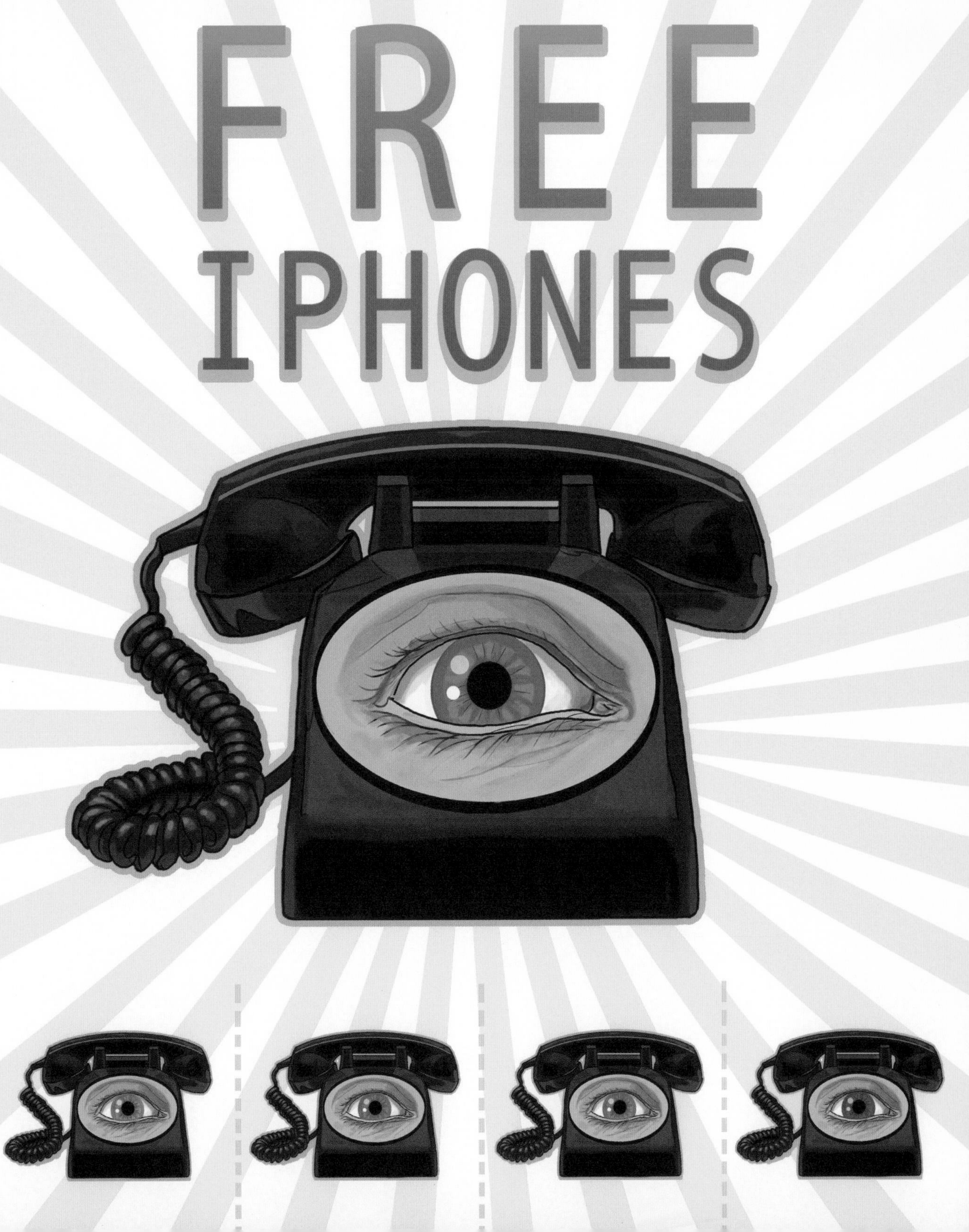
FREE
IPHONES

From the book *Should This Octopus Have Fewer Legs?* by PJ McQuade • Adams Media

SINGLE?

THINK YOU'RE A GOOD CATCH?
CAN'T STAY AFLOAT IN THE DATING POOL?
DON'T WORRY!

THERE ARE PLENTY OF
FISH IN THE SEA

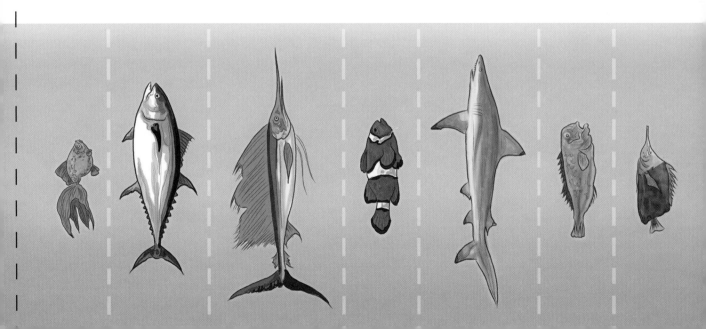

From the book *Should This Octopus Have Fewer Legs?* by PJ McQuade • Adams Media

WHO HAS A PIECE OF PAPER AND IS

AWESOME?

THIS GUY! THIS GUY! THIS GUY! THIS GUY! THIS GUY! THIS GUY! THIS GUY! THIS GUY!

From the book *Should This Octopus Have Fewer Legs?* by PJ McQuade • Adams Media

THE
END
IS
NIGH!

HEAVEN OR HELL? YOU DECIDE.

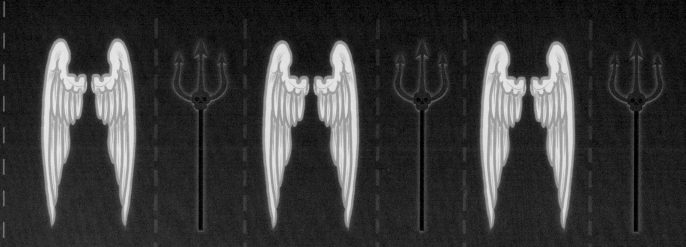

FREE
SLAP BRACELETS

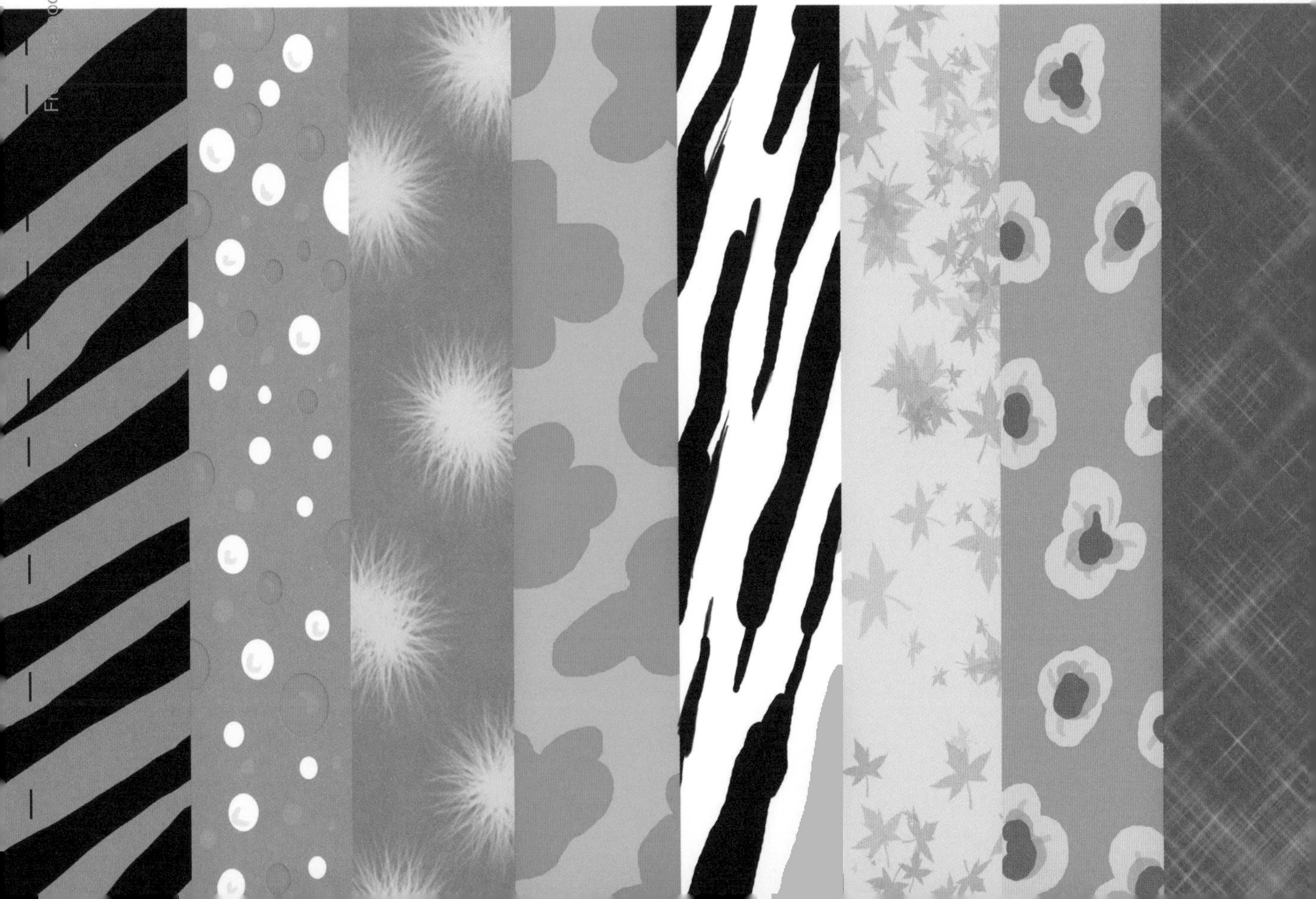

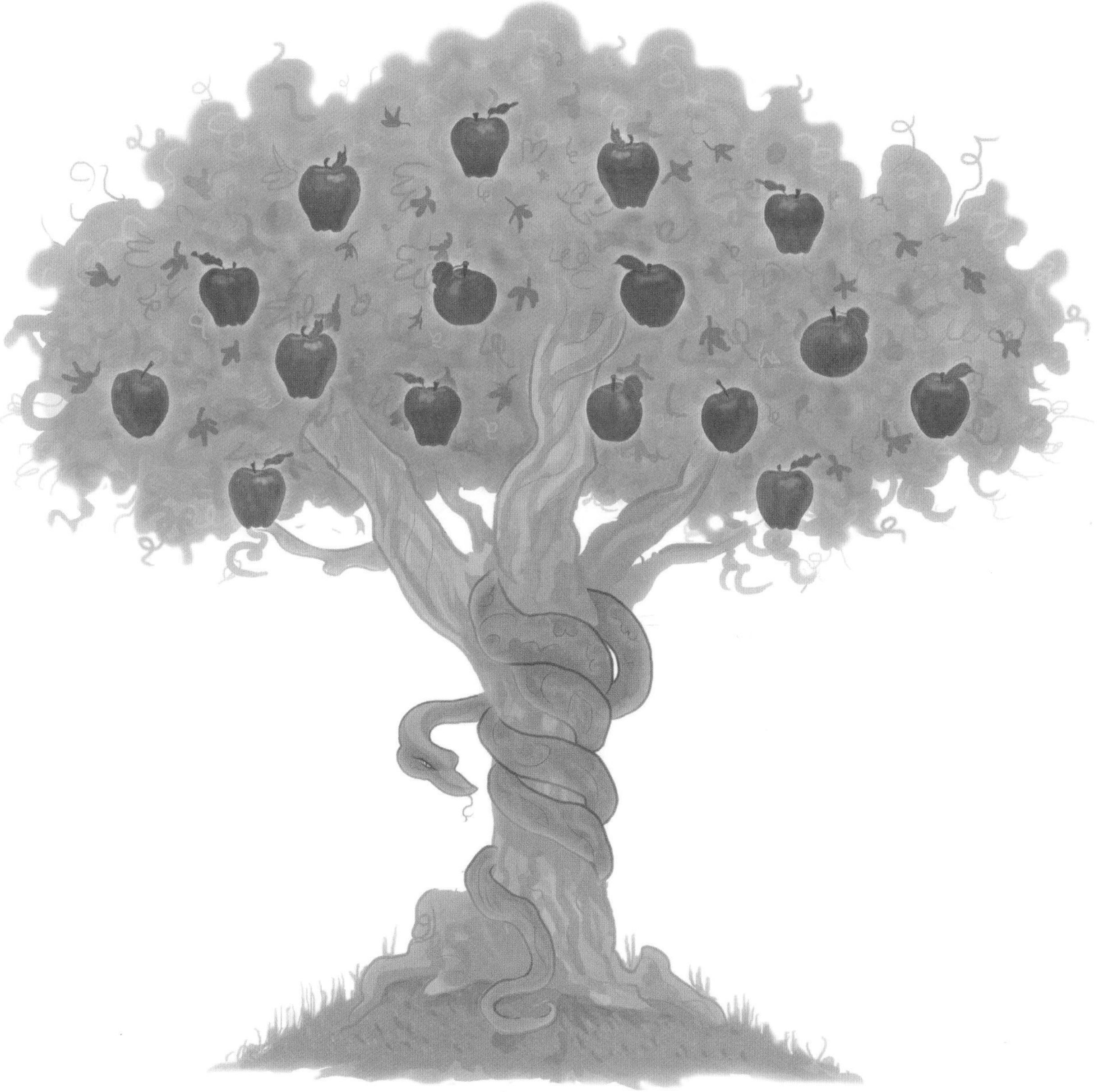

TEMPTED?

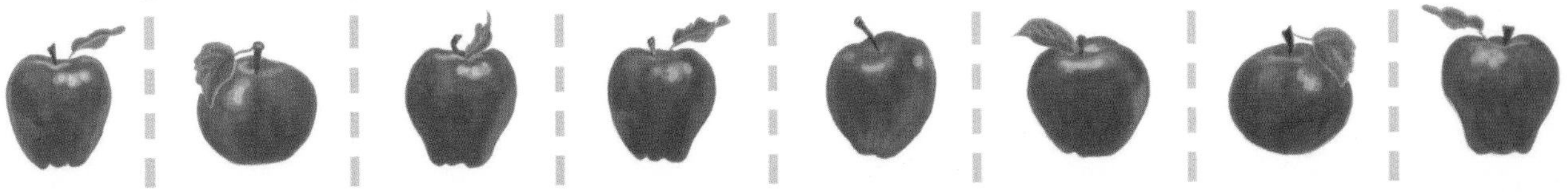

From the book *Should This Octopus Have Fewer Legs?* by PJ McQuade • Adams Media

Do you like

to waste paper?

yes *yes* *yes* *yes* *yes* *yes* *yes*

ABOUT THE AUTHOR

PJ McQuade lives in Brooklyn, New York, with his lovely wife Daria and their dog Football. He enjoys sleep masks, Steely Dan, Middle-earth, and magic beans. His clients have included the Syfy channel, *LA Weekly*, *Penthouse*, Beefeater Gin, MTV Press, and McSweeney's *Grantland*. His work has been honored by *Creative Review*, *Creative Quarterly*, and *American Illustration*. PJ is part of Illo Confidential, an exclusive art collective of twenty professional illustrators.

ACKNOWLEDGMENTS

Special thanks to my editor, Halli Melnitsky, who brought me in on this book and was absolutely wonderful to work with, and to all the good folks at Adams Media who helped during its creation—Karen Cooper, Meredith O'Hayre, Brendan O'Neill, Elisabeth Lariviere, Frank Rivera, Casey Ebert, and Chris Duffy.

To my loving family, immediate and extended, especially to my mom, Nancy; my father, Timothy; my sisters, Erin and Katie; my brother, Andrew; and grandmother, Mary. To my mother-in-law, Alexandra Sellon, and father-in-law, Michael Sellon.

To my dear friends, especially Steve Sallese, for his perfect ideas. To all the art teachers I've ever had. To Football, for being adorable. To my loving wife and partner, Daria, for believing in me and for being a constant source of inspiration. To the makers of things, to creators, to those who whittle and never tire.